My Little Gold◦ Jackie Robinson

By Frank J. Berrios

Illustrated by Betsy Bauer

The editors would like to thank James L. Gates Jr., Library Director, National Baseball Hall of Fame and Museum, for his assistance in the preparation of this book.

 A GOLDEN BOOK • NEW YORK

Library of Congress Control Number: 2017951349
ISBN 978-0-525-57868-0 (trade) — ISBN 978-0-525-57869-7 (ebook)
Printed in the United States of America
10 9 8 7 6 5 4 3 2

Jackie Robinson was a talented baseball player who became an American hero.

The first African American to play Major League Baseball in modern times, Jackie joined the Brooklyn Dodgers in 1947. In his first year, Jackie led the league in stolen bases, helped his team reach the World Series, and was named Rookie of the Year! Only two years later, he became the first black person to be honored as the National League's Most Valuable Player.

Jackie's full name was Jack Roosevelt Robinson. He was born in Georgia, the youngest of five children. Before Jackie's first birthday, his father left the family. Jackie never saw him again.

Jackie's mother, Mallie, moved the family to California, where she found work cleaning homes. Money was hard to come by, but Mallie was able to save enough to buy her family a house.

Jackie's sister, Willa Mae, looked after him while their mother worked. She even took little Jackie along when she started school! He was too young to sit in the classroom with her, so he played in the sandbox while his sister kept an eye on him through a window.

Jackie was always running, jumping, and playing. At school, he quickly made friends because he loved to play all types of sports. And Jackie hated to lose. Some kids would even give him their lunch if he promised to be on their team!

It wasn't easy for Jackie to grow up without
a dad. Now and then, he got into trouble. But
Jackie was smart, and he listened to the
caring grownups who gave him advice.
He also loved his mother very much
and wanted her to be proud of him.

Jackie became a star athlete in high school
tennis, football, baseball, basketball, and track!
He continued athletics in college, where he met
Rachel Isum, his future wife.

At this time, some states had segregation laws that kept black people and white people from living in the same neighborhoods, going to the same schools, and playing sports on the same teams. They couldn't even use the same public bathrooms or sit together on buses.

Because of segregation, black people who wanted to play baseball could only join teams in the Negro leagues.

After serving in the army, Jackie tried out for the Kansas City Monarchs—and easily made the team!

Playing in the Negro leagues was exciting, but there were long bus rides to and from the games. And the players often had to sleep and eat on the bus because most hotels and restaurants did not want to serve black people.

But things were about to change, thanks to Jackie . . . and a man named Branch Rickey.

Branch Rickey had seen white people mistreat black people all his life, and he hated it. Now, as general manager of the famous Brooklyn Dodgers, he would have a chance to make a stand. He decided it was time for black people and white people to play baseball together. And he knew Jackie Robinson was strong enough to lead the way.

Lots of people in baseball thought Branch Rickey was crazy. Some officials tried to keep Jackie from playing with white people by canceling games. The fans yelled from the stands and made fun of him.

Even some of Jackie's teammates treated him badly. But others, like shortstop Pee Wee Reese, stood by him when times were tough.

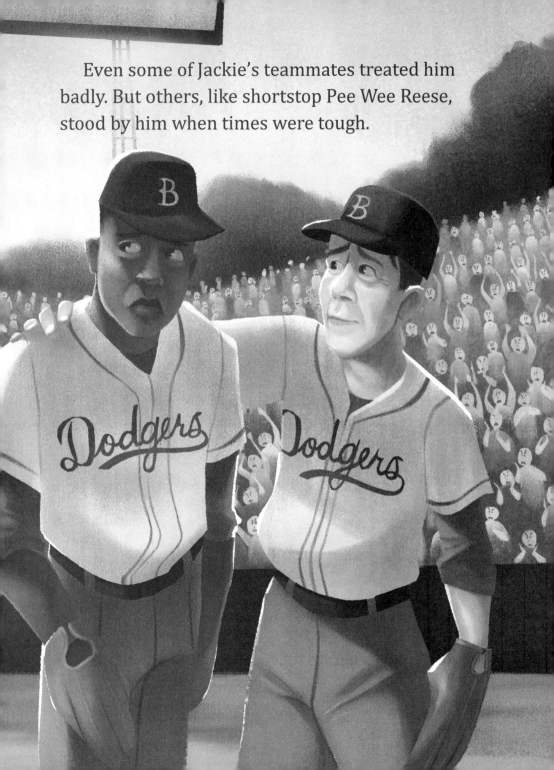

Nothing was going to stop Jackie from swinging his bat and stealing those bases. He led his team in singles, bunts, and runs scored.

And he helped his team win again and again
by making plays with lightning speed!

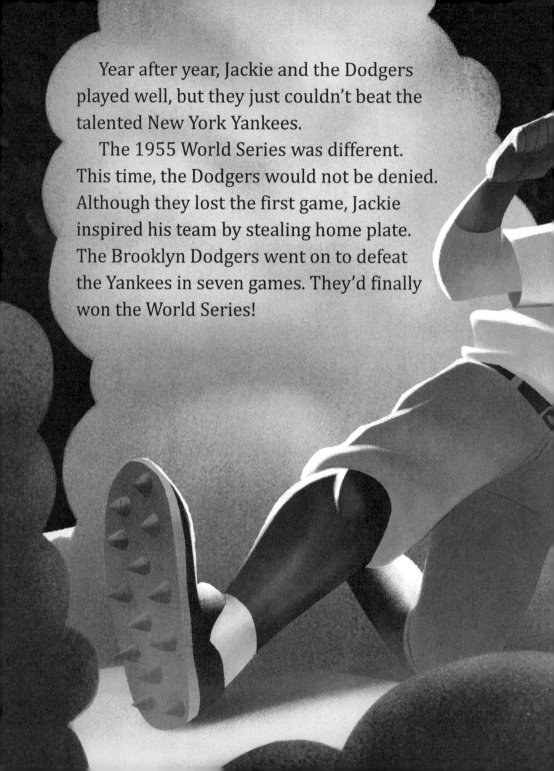

Year after year, Jackie and the Dodgers played well, but they just couldn't beat the talented New York Yankees.

The 1955 World Series was different. This time, the Dodgers would not be denied. Although they lost the first game, Jackie inspired his team by stealing home plate. The Brooklyn Dodgers went on to defeat the Yankees in seven games. They'd finally won the World Series!

"The Dodgers were a championship team because all of us had learned something," Jackie said later. "I had learned how to earn the respect of my teammates. They had learned that it's not skin color, but talent and ability that counts."

Jackie continued to play with the Dodgers for all of his ten seasons. During that time, players from other Negro leagues followed Jackie into the major leagues.

HIRE US

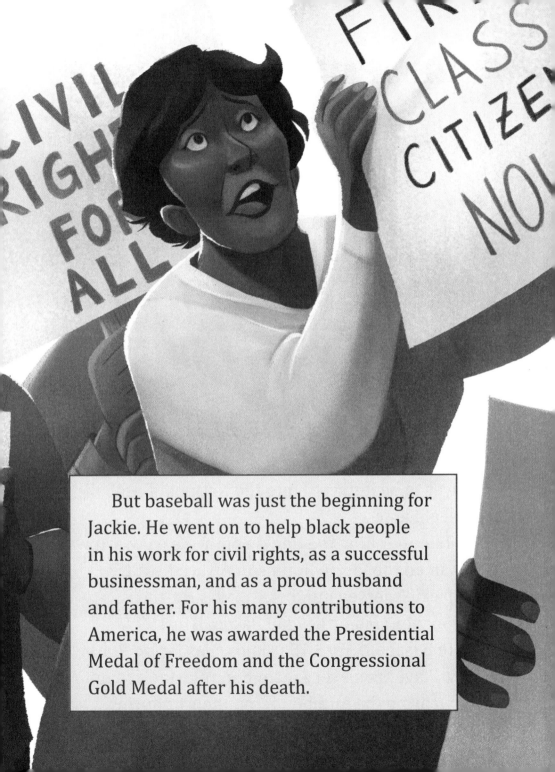

But baseball was just the beginning for Jackie. He went on to help black people in his work for civil rights, as a successful businessman, and as a proud husband and father. For his many contributions to America, he was awarded the Presidential Medal of Freedom and the Congressional Gold Medal after his death.

REMEMBERING JACKIE

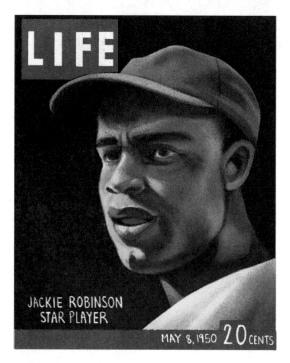

LIFE

JACKIE ROBINSON
STAR PLAYER

MAY 8, 1950 20 CENTS

In 1962, Jackie Robinson was the first black player to be inducted into the National Baseball Hall of Fame.

To honor him, the Rookie of the Year Award was renamed the Jackie Robinson Award in 1987.

Jackie's jersey number, 42, was retired throughout Major League Baseball in 1997.

In baseball, April 15 is known as Jackie Robinson Day. Players on every team honor Jackie's memory by wearing the number 42 on their uniforms.